Cover Characters: "the Way", "Flows (like a stream)"

Acknowledgements

Thank You to

my siblings & parents, Mike, the friendly producers,

all who I've read, namely Alan Watts,

my two dogs Moose & Luna,

the Garretón brothers,

& my love, Izzy,

For growing me in formative & formidable times.

•

•   •

•

•   •

•

•   •

•

•

Preface

When I started this booklet my working title was *Burn After Reading*, with obviously no thought to the 2008 film, but to underscore the non-seriousness and non-finality of this whole project — however it is *sincere* to the utmost. If you disagree, if you have a correction, any grievance, just light it on fire and watch your worries float away in ash. It *is* all okay.

I do not claim to have the ability to comprehensively express all that I write about here but I took the leap of doing this anyway, largely on the basis of a line from Alan Watts, where he says, "*It is not enough, anymore, to say: 'I say unto you..' no, you must put in your footnotes.*"[1] What he means of course is people are no longer taken sincerely when speaking from a place of simple intuition and feeling, they must have their footnotes of evidence, preferably handed down to them by some previously credentialed official.

This booklet, therefore, is my saying unto you. I have come to embrace my love of writing, and further have discovered the thrill of compiling and formatting that writing myself. This is, however, brief, and is meant only to put my foot in the door of the whole process.

As for the final title *Verbing*, it is, apart from this, recognized as a system of adding the *-ing*

---

[1]Found in Watts' lecture, "*On Being God*", minute 1:20

suffix onto almost any word to create action nouns (i.e. the galaxy is 'planeting'; an apple tree is 'appleing'; and so on). This way of talking about the world makes everything seem to come alive, and reminds you that it is all involved in an ever-changing symbiotic system. My thought as I chose it as my title was: "We are all Verbing thus" — we are all *happening thus;* we are all *doing thus* — in this Eternal Now.

     With all that said, I hope the reader enjoys.

..and don't forget to burn after reading.

Helvetia, Oregon
June 12th, 2017

                          Jacob Roloff

"Our days are precious but we gladly see them
going
If in their place a thing more precious growing;
A rare, exotic plant, our gardener's heart delighting;
A child whom we are teaching, a booklet we are
writing."

The Glass Bead Game,
by Hermann Hesse, page 414

Part 1

● ● ● ● Ignorance

"Verily I say to you, unless you are converted and become like children, you will not enter the kingdom of heaven."
Matthew 18:3

For a long time I separated my life, without *consciously* knowing, into two main categories: self and influence, as if the two were distinct from each other. I then split my life into three stages: Pre-film, Peri-film, and Post-film, all with the categories of self distinct from influence within them.

I've always taken that Pre-film period as sort of a pristine example of what life *could've been,* or kept on being; exploring the wonderland that is my family property, eating fresh picked fruits for all three meals, campfires as often as we could fit them in, company retreats—rewarding us with as many snow cones as we could stomach, and dozens of other activities that are the hallmark of my growing up. Obviously, I didn't expect those specific activities to go on forever, but it *seemed* to me that my ability to enjoy them and have them naturally evolve into something new but equally innocent was cut short.

I now know that this illusion, kept up for nearly 20 years, of "My" life being "altered" by "outside" influences is just that: an illusion. At whatever age separates the Pre- and Peri- stages of film, I had it in my mind that something had been changed. But what? Was there really an underlying reality that was somehow missed, some script of life that had been improvised and sabotaged? Was this just a botched attempt at the real thing?

What would my life look like if I had had a different life, different influences, tragedies, joys, hobbies. . . what a meaningless question I've found that to be! I am, this!

I *am* my influences and also the one influenced, because what else *could* I be? There is no Plan A that had a wrench thrown in and becomes Plan B; it's just *The* Plan (perhaps plan being a poor choice of metaphor). In plainer words: I, as Jacob Roloff and as an ego, did not *possess* any life before the one I'm experiencing now that is being altered whatsoever. Now is I. Knowing, of course, that when the past or future happens or happened, it is in the Now of that moment.

So, I was going along at, say, 4, with a relatively average life, and then all of a sudden certain things start to come to my awareness, like my dad having built a cowboy town, castle, and massive tree fort right in the backyard. Then further on from that, falling off my bike, cracking my head open. A little on from that, a TV crew arrives to start documenting my family. All this, and a great deal more, makes up me in *this* Now, and there is no relevance to the question, "What would I be, had (x) not happened?", other than as an end to waking yourself up from that particularly strong illusion that you are separate from life. You're not.

People think their lives have been driven off course by good and bad circumstances, but what life has been driven? I think they are assuming statistical averages as real facts. If they don't meet the average standard for whatever, then something has gone awry. For instance, the average lifespan of a person living in the United States is around 75. If a person dies before that they call it premature, but premature only to what the numbers say, not reality. Because saying that *what is happening now* is premature makes little to no sense. It's now; how you are going to handle it is the question.

There is a certain element of ignorance in childhood where you feel that things commonly understood as mundane are instead rather significant. It's why children can play with cardboard boxes and stare at ants and other insects for hours, and how they can pretend a model airplane is the real deal with noises that seem to jump out of their mouths, like *bbzzzzrrrrrrr*, there it is! the plane right here in my hand! It's extraordinary. This feeling, taken to the next (or rather, previous) level is apparent in infants as well. Freud called it the Oceanic Feeling or Oceanic Effect, and it describes the sensation of connectedness between everything. It's a lack of feeling "I". A baby doesn't know that it is separate from the outside world until probably around the time of ceasing breastfeeding, according to Freud. Only then, after this unified process of crying and feeding ends, does it realize that breast is other and *I* am *I*.

Very quickly we start learning things, and how to function properly as a person, as an ego and I experience. Incidentally the word ego is I think very misused. People say, "that person has gotten quite a big head. Very egotistical." But ego doesn't mean arrogance or conceit — it is literally the sensation of I, which all living things have. And if someone were to submit unyieldingly to that sensation, as in all other sensations, it can be abused. This leads to arrogant behaviors, as well as greed and casual disconnection with nature and everything else, but ego isn't those behaviors, it is a tool used poorly. *"When the wrong man uses the right means, the right means work in the wrong way."*[2]

So before we learn about *things* as distinct from *I* we feel inherently connected to everything in a sort of divine, glorious ignorance — *ignorance is bliss*, as they say. And after learning of so many things a new strain of ignorance comes into play which is not knowing the history of this tool called ego and how it developed in you.

---

[2] *The Secret of the Golden Flower: A Chinese Book of Life,* 1962, Carl Gustav Jung and Richard Wilhelm

This new, different level of learned ignorance is what Matthew 18:3 is speaking to when Jesus says, *"..unless you are converted and become like children, you will not enter the kingdom of heaven."* If you hold too tight to "I" and become too engrossed with your own image of yourself, you'll be stuck forever in the struggle of self against other. Your image versus reality. Your image of you versus you in God's image.

So, ignorance *is* bliss; though, also, in another stage, very much the opposite. We talk about ignorance and much else while forgetting that evolution takes place on all scales micro and macro, and if those be up and down, also left and right. Everything is evolving in one way individually, and in another as completely integral to the group evolution. So, when one is ignorant to *things* through the Oceanic Effect, it doesn't go away but evolves, and so survives in a different form — that is, "adult", or simply learned ignorance.

It's a funny thing then, when evolution of thought, body, culture, religion, feeling, mountains.. the ten thousand things.. flows swiftly on and people still try to scoop a cup of the streaming to classify it. Just hold on, wait a while. . . take another, and what else do you see?

Panta rhei — Everything flows.

The same man, Heraclitus, says this, too:
   "You could not step twice into the same river; for other waters are ever flowing on to you."

Part 2

● ● ● ● Frustration

"Man suffers only because he takes seriously what the gods made for fun."
Alan Watts

This is the part people tell me they most expect to hear and thus I am least enthusiastic to share: being filmed and my thoughts. Whenever I talk about it I see people say and stories titled, "Jacob reveals..", as if it is *serious* or definitive in any sense. I use serious in the same sense as asking if a particular disease is "serious"—is it definite, is it life-threatening, world-altering—and this is not. Having said that, I'll go on...

When I was around 6 years old my family started appearing on a reality show, then-titled *Little People, Big Dreams*. This ushered in a new era for me personally, my family in general, and the awareness of little people as a whole.

The first few years of doing this show were pretty alright, just a few (dozen) extra people around the house and farm. The actual filming in that beginning period was subject to the events unfolding, that is, something happened *then* the cameras came running. After the few first years of testing the waters, the whole process did a sort of flip where events became subject to the filming, that is, became more orchestrated than spontaneous, in a weird indistinguishable mix. That phase went on for a while, too, until turning into the dominantly orchestrated ordeal it is today.

I remember near the beginning I rather liked the whole thing. There was a certain day that is stuck in my memory where our parents let us all cash in a portion of whatever money we were receiving at the time, and I remember going to Toys R Us and Barnes and Noble and some other stores and being so excited while thinking, "This is alright after all." Of course, I didn't have the wherewithal then to know any misgivings I might have later on about the whole thing, but when I think back to that day, I'm *sure* that that is what was going through my mind, given how positively I remember it.

There have been so many monetary and material benefits from the show, it's become hard to express my dislike of other aspects without accusations flooding in of my failure to appreciate what I've been privileged to experience. It's just simply not the case that criticism cancels appreciation. I appreciate the office of the Presidency, and criticism is at the same time required and necessary for proper function of office. Now I'll expand on my thoughts of these material benefits weighed against what I thought was the expense of an "innocently experienced childhood". .

I have that in quotes because, as alluded to in a point I made above, what life was there to be defiled and stolen of innocence? No life, because, if it must be said, the theft of innocence was but a stage of the same life that I've been living since the beginning. However, I've just come to this realization fairly recently, so I'll continue with that implicitly in mind.

When I reflect on my childhood, I have really only a small collection of memories before the filming started, and so it is, reasonably, a large chunk of what I think about day-to-day and what I credit for having the most influence on me psychologically as a child. Chiefly and simply, it forced me to grow up faster than normal (whatever a normal rate may be). Doing on-the-fly interviews and formal ones alike forced me to answer certain questions about myself, my family, and my life that I normally might not have wondered about for some years. That was a sort of forced self-consciousness, meant literally, consciousness of self. I was constantly reflecting and analyzing life and things happening around me — not always to be prepared for interviews, but due to my own curiosity which perhaps sprung from the prodding of such interviews.

In this way I see the positive and negative aspects of filming flip on a dime; on the one hand, I'm stuck in front of a lens, symbolizing the millions of people that watch(ed) our show, left to my own devices of coping and getting attention that usually panned out great for The Brass in LA. On the other hand, instantly, it forced me to evolve mentally way faster than I would have, I think, under circumstances of less pressure. This is regarding the interview ordeal, but to zoom in on the specific issue of my accelerated mental development, it also has its own set of positive and negative sides flipping on a dime — that is, contrasting yet connected.

On the one hand my critical thinking and contemplative abilities were intensely practiced and strengthened. On the other, I felt isolated, and due to that, angry. Isolated because I had such a sheer amount of information processing in my brain that I could not well just spit out an explanation or synopsis to someone and 'vent'. This led to arguments and miscommunications with family, especially my parents, culminating really in their decision to experiment having me see a therapist. Well, that simply exercised my stubborn adolescent ability to stay quiet and stay put — great practice for the form of meditation I've discovered called *zazen* — and led to all the more misplaced anger and frustration.

It's difficult to convey the rift that grew between my family and I without morphing into a groveling tell-all. I will leave you with but a few bullet points of the situations my mental overhaul wreaked: daily encounters with my mom ending with anything but a smile, having little to no relationship with my siblings, locking myself away in my room for all hours of the day, except to relieve myself or to unthankfully grab some food my mom had made. I was truly the epitome of a stereotypical teenager — a description which I was given frequently — fanning the flames of this frustrated state of mind. I could kindly describe it now as a mental "updating"; I was useless, even a hindrance, and a shell, just as a computer is when you have to update it's software. Luckily the damage and whatever hurt I caused was not too far-reaching or permanent, for all those problems have been mended in recent years.

This frustration came way after my own oceanic effect and well into my learned ignorance of where my self-sensation came from. Illusion as regards to Self might make some people queasy so I think a better word is convention. Conventions are ideas, and as such, are massively influential, however, with no concrete reality (i.e. equator, inches, even money). We use conventions to make life easier by collectively agreeing (consciously or unconsciously) on certain fundamental systems to create a sort of common denominator for things like communication, travel, and commerce. We may have different names for money, but Money is the fundamental concept— dollars, pounds, and pesos are just facets. Indeed you can see money and it *seems* concrete and real-ly influential, but the value and power of it is entirely up to us, and on this collective agreement, it is worth quite a lot. Even too much, for we have forgotten as a society that it is a conventional symbol and has no real value beyond what we collectively have given it. This isn't a practical how-to on escaping the trap of money or lack of; this is observational. Alan Watts has a perfect metaphor about this confusion[3] of convention for reality. He tells of a construction crew building a building. The person who contracted them comes along to find that they've stopped working, and asks why, to which the workers reply, "Sorry, we've run out of inches. We can't go on with the job." It's ridiculous!

Now take the principle of that to the real world where someone (everyone) comes along and says, "Excuse me, why aren't we feeding the hungry peoples of the world?" To which the powers that be reply: "Sorry. We haven't got enough money." It's really the same situation. It's all there, the resources and actual product, the technologies and agricultural skill; all that's missing is our clear heads. We're all muddied up with symbols we don't realize are symbols. It's a mess! And this basic problem causes a lot, if not *all,* of the worlds frustrations.

I allowed myself to be in such a frustrated state of mind for a long time, until hitting a wall of reason knowing that there *must* be another way. I retreated just a little bit further into seclusion with books, and cultivation of intellect and mind. These too, I have learned, are just tools. Tools for finding a sense of self, love, and respect for others, and appreciation for reality — which you then realize

---

3Found in Watts' lecture, "Veil of Thoughts", minute 4:00.

has been there all along, waiting, whereafter you can cease cultivation and enjoy the dance of the moment. This searching through further abstraction is like searching for misplaced car keys that end up being found in your back pocket. Some genuine anger might come up in the feverish and desperate search, and you think of some really clever ways and spots to look. When found though, and upon realizing it was hidden right under your nose all along, you let out a good laugh and all is well. So it is with a search for self and reality. You might, on the way, be misled, fooled, or frustrated, but it will pass as everything does and your search will not be for nothing. You need only resist submission to frustration and have faith. It will take you right to the edge, and just as you think it's time to give in, the pressure will be released.

In my story, as in many others for thousands of years, this is where Zen comes in. Zen is sometimes titled a philosophy or religion but it's really a "way of liberation", a pointing — at direct experience.

Part 3

• • • • Revelations

"If you are unable to find the truth right where you are, where else do you expect to find it?"
Dogen

As I understand it, philosophy is the love and search for wisdom, and religion is the search for meaning and truth. I have found, or experienced rather, that the Christianity taught to me was too distracted with itself to have time for such a search, and too busy policing the search to enjoy it. There was no fun or lightheartedness in the Christianity I experienced, just solemnity, seriousness, and damnation. It wasn't until I discovered the old mystics, like St. Francis, Meister Eckhart, St. Thomas, and Dionysius, who were of course officially denounced as "un-Christian", that I saw first-hand there was indeed a facet of Christianity that was curious and playful.

These men had more in common with Far East religions (called so for convenience) than with the officialdom of the Church. Through Alan Watts' writings on Zen Buddhism I found them, and found also G.K. Chesterton, who is fairly contemporary and who wrote things like, "The angels fly because they take themselves lightly"[4], and had a general attitude of deep appreciation and surprise at the world. The type of attitude that births those troublesome curiosities and outsider tendencies not so appreciated by the average dutiful churchgoer.

I became like that, and had no interest being scowled at and distracted by quarrels over traditional behavior, for I had also in my mind the motto of the Royal Society: *Nullius in verba* — On the word of no one. In other words, think and discover for yourself. So, I reconnected with my love of books, reading about the mysteries and misconceptions of: Zen, Hinduism, Karma, God, Morality, Mystical Christianity, Cosmic Consciousness, and all sorts of other avenues of psychology, philosophy, and religion with authors ranging from Arthur C. Clarke, to Terrence McKenna, to Dante Alighieri, to C.G. Jung, to Chomsky, to Nikos Kazantzakis, to William James, and of course, Alan Watts — with so many left unnamed. I absolutely plummeted in love with books again, and when I become interested in something I tenaciously pursue it 'til the end — which in the case of books is infinity.

One of the key things I've learned that has been formative in my personal philosophy is the redefinition of karma. People use it as a shorthand

---

[4]*Orthodoxy*, 1908, G. K. Chesterton

term for the principle of cause and effect but karma is not so much a billiard game where bad things become bad rewards, and vice versa with good, as it is simply an expression of responsibility.

Karma means 'your doing', except the you in that definition is not you as your ego-name, but the deep down you that is this whole universe. The you that you are not aware of, the you that grows your fingernails and pumps your blood. Just as trees of specific species all appear and in some sense are individual (one can die and the rest live on), they are more importantly a part of one larger system, one larger unity. That underlying unity-form is the 'you that does' in karma. So as I pretend to be frustrated by any grievances I have with filming, I soon realize that it is my karma and my doing. It's just me... nothing to be scared of or angry about.

This realization has been pivotal to my finding peace. It's funny, as I say that I've 'found peace' I think of what else there was... really just me pretending to be worked up — willingly putting on a mask of frustration and ignorance.

Now here I am again putting on a mask of 'peacefulness', but that is not the Truth either, just a stage, albeit a more pleasant one to live through on this plane of existence. As with everything, it passes. I am sailing in calm seas now, evading as well as heading towards a storm. But that is the beauty, isn't it? The highs, the lows, the love, the heartache, the crests and the troughs on the wave of life. If it wasn't this way everything would be a flat, even, uneventful bore. There would be no wigglyness to the game! and that is after all why we love staring off into the ocean and resting our eyes on faraway mountains: they're chalk-full of wiggly beauty and unpredictability. That element is an essential part of life, it's why we humans have free will after all; a mountain could blow its top off, the ocean could whip up a giant wave, and humans could "*borrow from the heavens a tongue, so to curse them more at leisure.*"[5]

Speaking of the heavens, I want to talk about my thoughts and discoveries in that regard. I was born and raised in a Christian household, a Christian school, and a Christian country. There are hundreds of years of ideas about God piled up behind where I find myself now. As I was growing up and thinking whatever I thought about that particular religion, one thing was for sure: God was from the Bible. That may seem obvious, but is the Bible where he stops?

Just for a moment, take away all images and preconceived thoughts you have of God. Now.. God — G-O-D — is just a word to describe a concept. The concept is "the one without a second" — duality transcended — the Primordial creation principle. The Bible talks much about him, and because I and the majority of my readers are so immersed in this Christian society, He has been almost exclusively associated with the one religion and book. But isn't it strange we confine him to

---

[5]From G. K. Chesterton's poem, "*The Fish*"

such things as specific books and morals? How could he be only present in the Bible, and not so present in the Qur'an or the Tao Te Ching? After all, is God not the one without a second? How can he be this and not that? Is there not within him good and evil, positive and negative, combined as one in divine harmony? Everything we can *think* of is not God and neither is it's opposite; the God that is good without evil is a mere image, and an idolatrous one at that.

For he is ultimately not He or One, but no-He and no-One. Neither is he Moral or Immoral, but no-Moral. "Blasphemy!", says you. Well I say...duality is the language of this world we experience, and God, having cultivated this world, cultivated also duality and so is 'outside' of it, and because of that, is at once *inside* of everything — this is the meaning of the Incarnation. God is here and now, just let him through! For if you affirm he *is* outside you affirm also that he is *not* inside, trapping him again in duality. This is the trickiness of talking about God in clear terms. We can't. Words are part of this world, no?, then how should we talk about God and his nature (or Kingdom) adequately? Well, let me remind you of mustard seeds... You have to understand though, when Jesus spoke of the mustard seed, there was not the luxury of libraries of commentaries on it; he just said unto them, and although we have the word parable to describe it, I think he was speaking simply and sincerely. He was answering a question of the Eternal God and Kingdom with the story of a mustard seed bound in time and duality, for he realized that that is all we *can* do! It's a funny sort of paradoxical answer you see all the time in Zen and Buddhist stories between masters and their students.

This unreachable character of the Eternal by clear instructions and teaching is what the Zen story of the finger pointing at the Moon is about. And just to clarify, there are many parallels between the meaning of language in these religions; among them, to name a few: Buddha could be substituted for God, Kingdom of God for nirvana or enlightenment, sin for suffering, and so on; please don't take offense or cry blaspheme on account of mere words symbolizing God but not being the real thing. As the Zen story goes:

Monk: *Please explain to me these scriptures.*

Hui-Neng: *Sorry, but I can't read the words. Read to me these scriptures and I will be able to understand them.*

Monk: *How can you understand the scriptures if you cannot read the words?*

Hui-Neng : *The truth and the words are two different things. The words can be compared with a finger. We can show the moon with a finger, but the finger is not the moon. To look at the moon means to look over the finger. The words are like a finger pointing* *towards the truth. Generally speaking, we see only the finger. The truth abide over the finger.*[6]

For a long time I thought I had to leave religion because the material was inconsistent with what I inherently felt, but then I realized that it was the way people are thinking and talking *about* it that I don't jive with. This is what people mean when they say they were taught, or even more severely, indoctrinated, by their parents into a certain religion. This is partly true, but religion means only the way of *thinking* about this Ultimate Reality, which becomes normalized and evolved over hundreds of years with the parents as products of the same sort of indoctrination process. The essence of the Truth is there always! but it cannot be taught to you — anything taught is again bound in duality — God only *knows*, God only *is*. Nevertheless we become fish swimming in water, unaware of how it could be any different, for the water just *is* — and being taught to know is what is for us. It's a very exciting thing, though, evolving likewise as fish once did, and stepping onto a new plane of understanding. Religion's purpose should be that of the older fish in the story who swims along and says, "Morning boys, how's the water?". To which we say in curiosity, "What the hell is water?" Lacking, though, the curiosity and contemplation, you swim around

---

[6]http://www.taopage.org/huineng/anecdmlote.ht

angry for-ever, championing always the tried and true method of putting it off by saying, "It's just how it works." Have some curiosity and wonder *for God's sake!*

I realized finally this thing: that religion, and likewise all other symbols, are just stepping stones to a *higher* knowing; that the actual scripture and all you've heard about it is still up to interpretation and is in danger always of human error — *Nullius in verba — experience suchness for yourself.* Come to think of it, this state of higher knowing is less that, and more so a higher *un*knowing (for historical context on this idea I encourage you to read the 14th century book *The Cloud of Unknowing*, whose author is unknown [o, the poetry], but whose text still holds much weight in mystical Christianity.)

This distinction between the word religion and it's institution, and the meaning behind it of being a mere stepping stone, is pivotal understanding when I say I choose not to call myself a Christian, or a Zen Buddhist, but have full faith in the truths available in them, and other religions. I have found my vocation in Zen and Christianity, others find them elsewhere and all is still well. Why waste time trying to pin down and capture what is ever changing and flowing onwards?

Just watch the river flowing! "Worry not for the morrow," and join in its babbling laughter . . .

Further reading

by **Dionysius the Areopagite**:
- Theologia Mystica

by **G.K. Chesterton**:
- Orthodoxy
- St. Thomas Aquinas and St. Francis of Assisi

by **Hermann Hesse**:
- Siddartha
- The Glass Bead Game (*Magister Ludi*)

by **William James**:
- The Varieties of Religious Experience
- The Philosophy of William James (Modern Library)

by **Nikos Kazantzakis**:
- The Greek Passion

by **Lao-tzu**:
- Tao te Ching (*Daodejing*)

by **Terence McKenna, Rupert Sheldrake, & Ralph Abraham**:
- The Evolutionary Mind
- Chaos, Creativity, and Cosmic Consciousness

by **Alan Watts**:
- Behold the Spirit
- The Way of Zen
- Psychotherapy East & West
- Out of Your Mind
- Nature, Man and Woman

Made in the USA
Lexington, KY
02 January 2018